CHINA
Coloring Book

DISCOVER THESE COLORING PAGES
FOR KIDS TO HAVE FUN COMPLETING

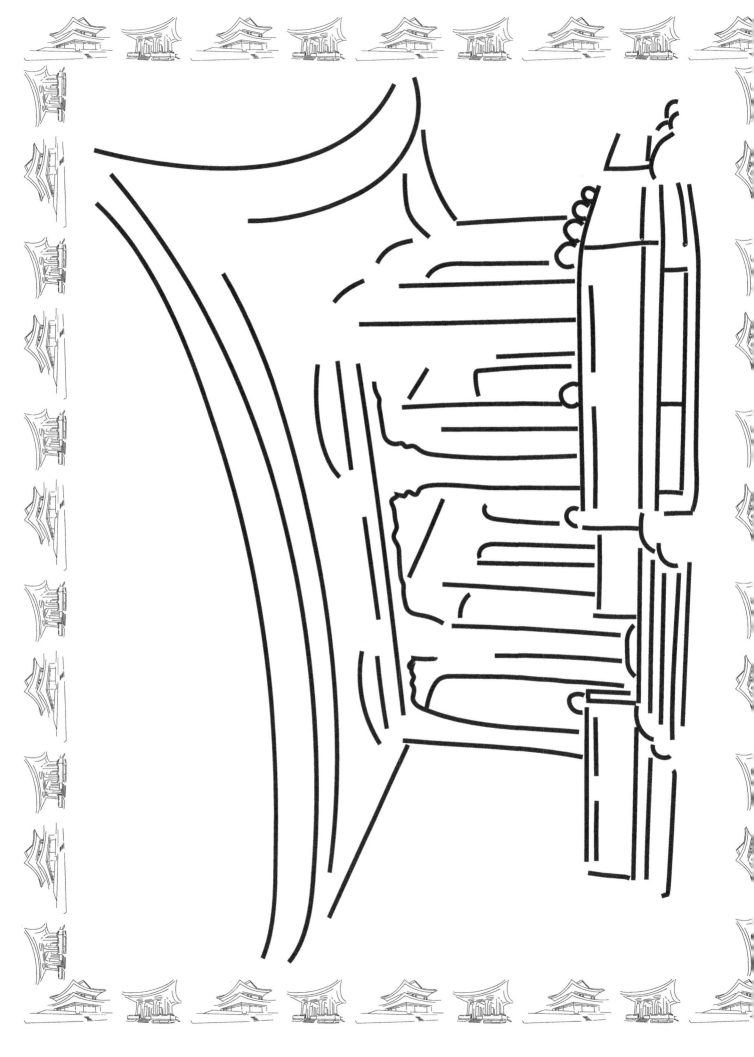

This is a Bleed Through Page If You Are Using a Coloring Marker or Pen!

Bold Illustrations
COLORING BOOKS

This is a Bleed Through Page If You Are Using a Coloring Marker or Pen!

Bold Illustrations
COLORING BOOKS

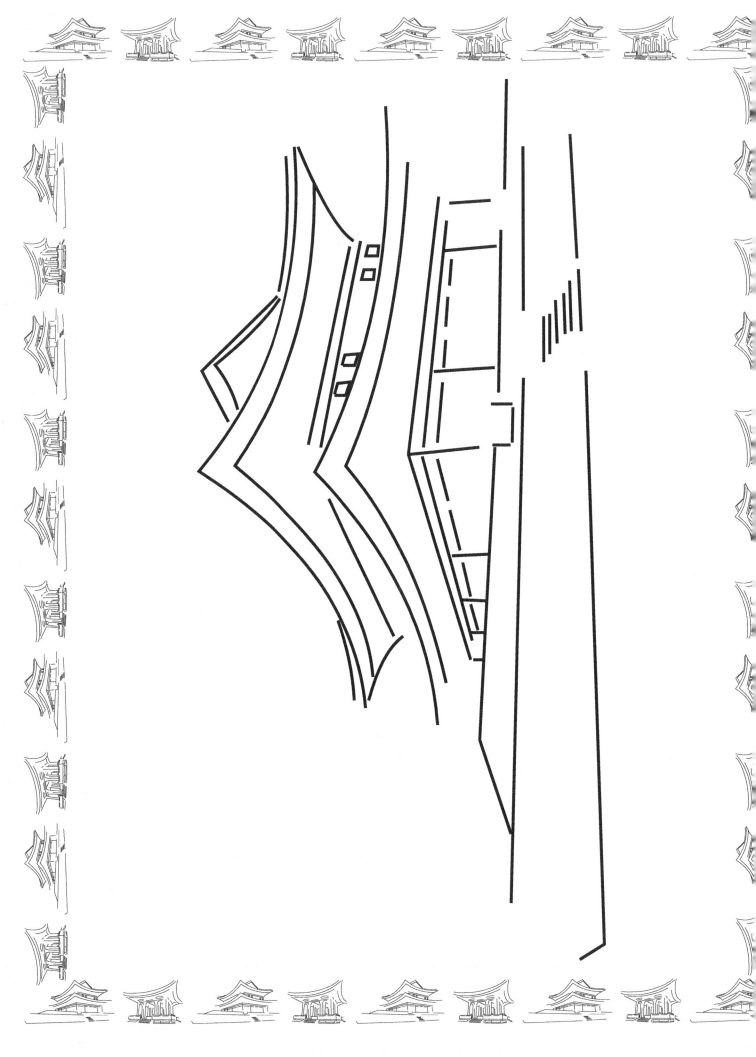

This is a Bleed Through Page If You Are Using a Coloring Marker or Pen!

Bold Illustrations

COLORING BOOKS

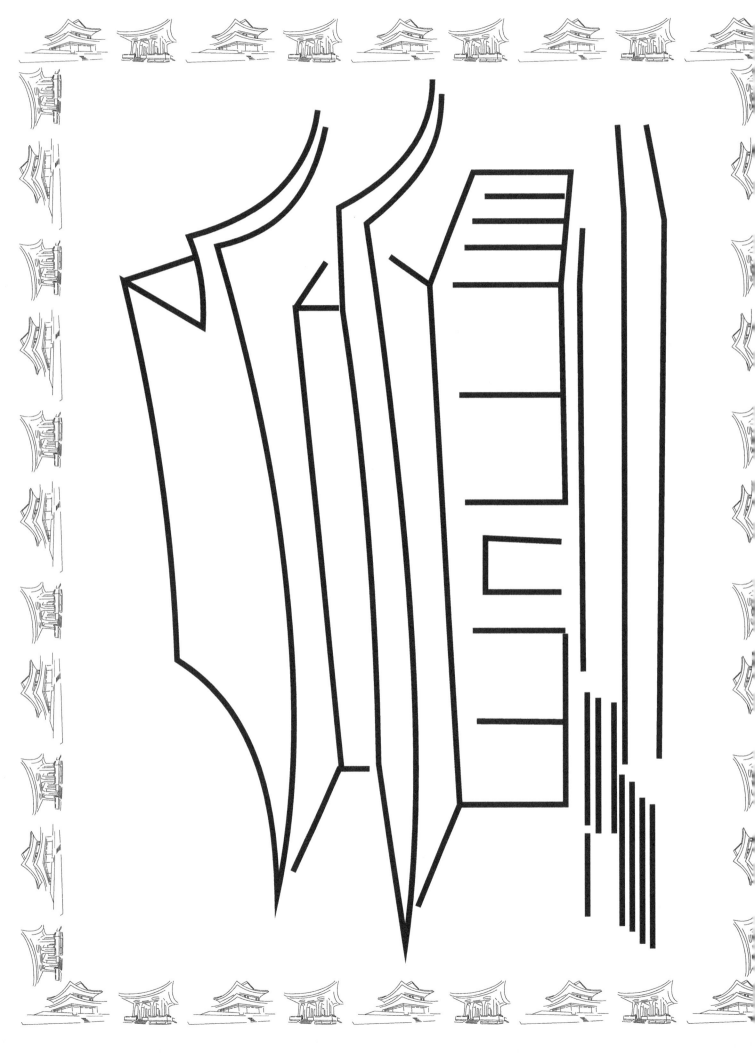

This is a Bleed Through Page If You Are Using a Coloring Marker or Pen!

Bold Illustrations
COLORING BOOKS

This is a Bleed Through Page If You Are Using a Coloring Marker or Pen!

Bold Illustrations

COLORING BOOKS

This is a Bleed Through Page If You Are Using a Coloring Marker or Pen!

Bold Illustrations
COLORING BOOKS

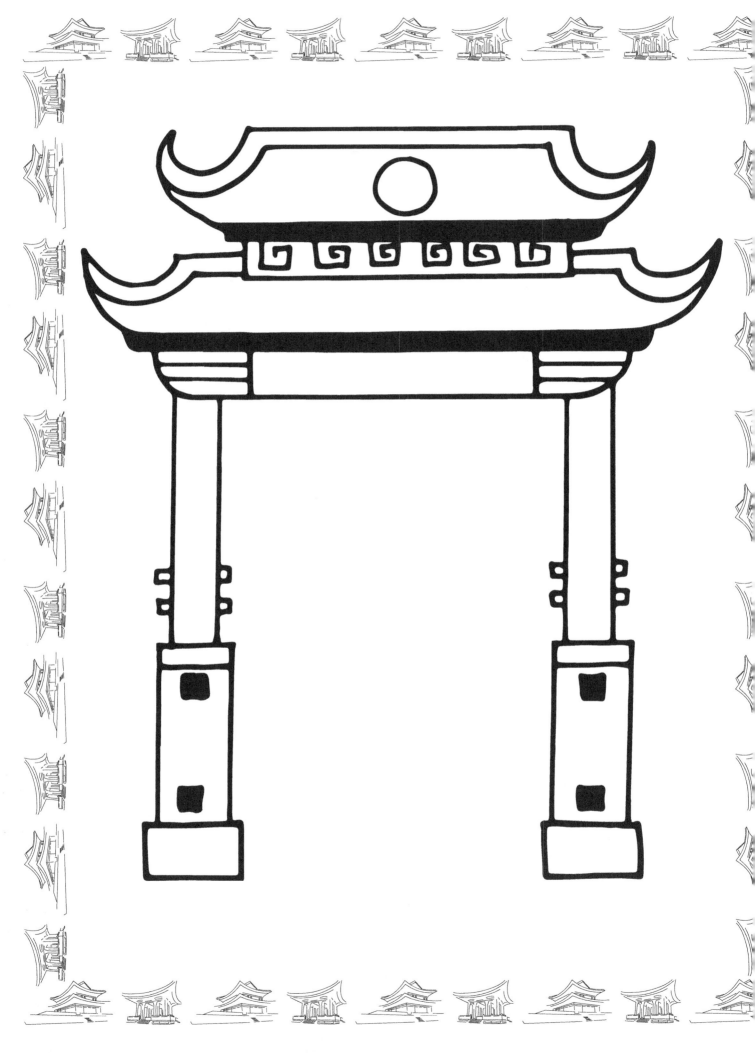

Bold Illustrations
COLORING BOOKS

This is a Bleed Through Page If You Are Using a Coloring Marker or Pen!

Bold Illustrations
COLORING BOOKS

Bold Illustrations
COLORING BOOKS

This is a Bleed Through Page If You Are Using a Coloring Marker or Pen!

Bold Illustrations
COLORING BOOKS

This is a Bleed Through Page If You Are Using a Coloring Marker or Pen!

Bold Illustrations
COLORING BOOKS

This is a Bleed Through Page If You Are Using a Coloring Marker or Pen!

Bold Illustrations
COLORING BOOKS

This is a Bleed Through Page If You Are Using a Coloring Marker or Pen!

Bold Illustrations
COLORING BOOKS

Bold Illustrations

COLORING BOOKS

This is a Bleed Through Page If You Are Using a Coloring Marker or Pen!

Bold Illustrations

COLORING BOOKS

This is a Bleed Through Page If You Are Using a Coloring Marker or Pen!

Bold Illustrations
COLORING BOOKS

This is a Bleed Through Page If You Are Using a Coloring Marker or Pen!

Bold Illustrations
COLORING BOOKS

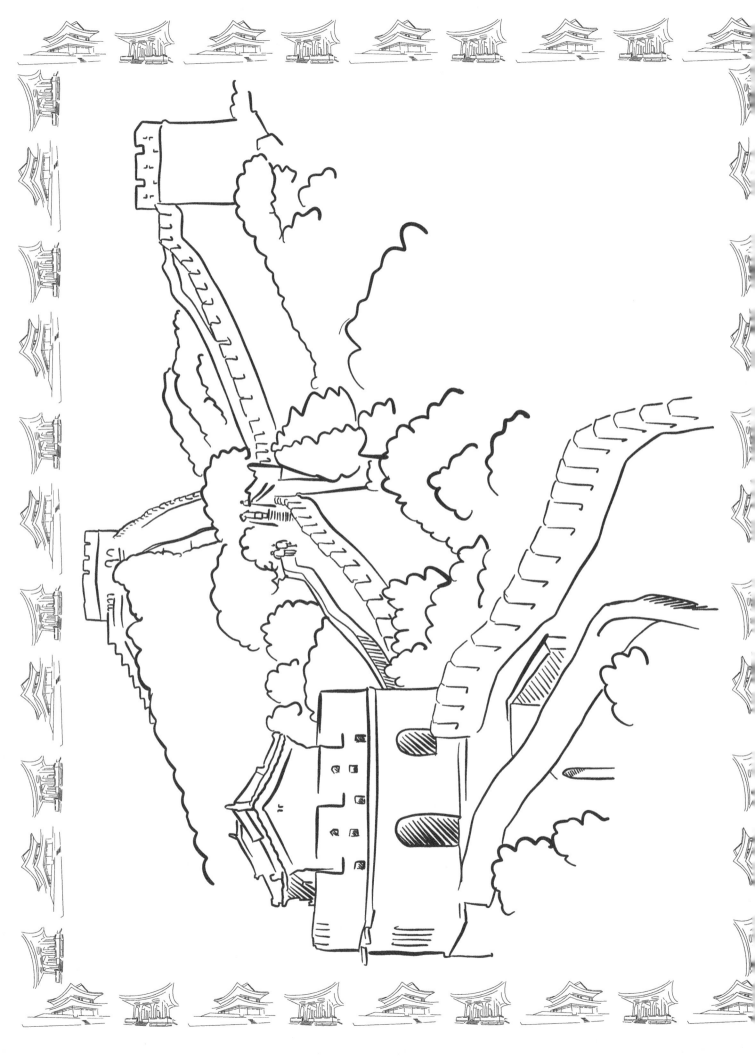

Bold Illustrations

COLORING BOOKS

This is a Bleed Through Page If You Are Using a Coloring Marker or Pen!

Bold Illustrations
COLORING BOOKS

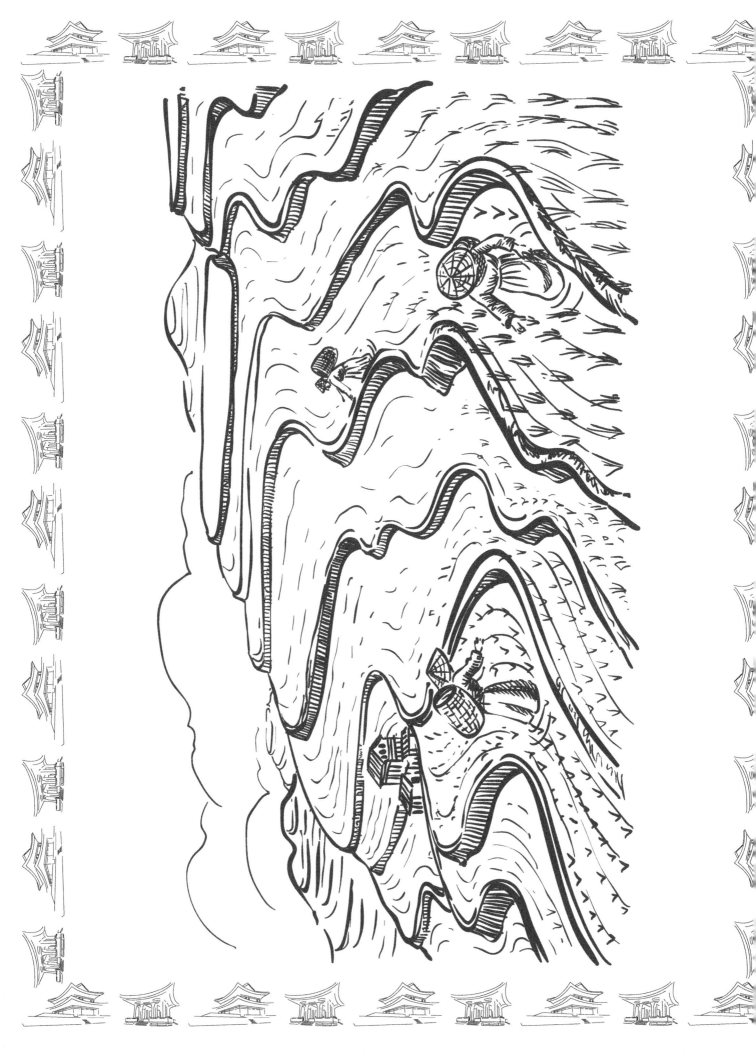

This is a Bleed Through Page If You Are Using a Coloring Marker or Pen!

Bold Illustrations
COLORING BOOKS

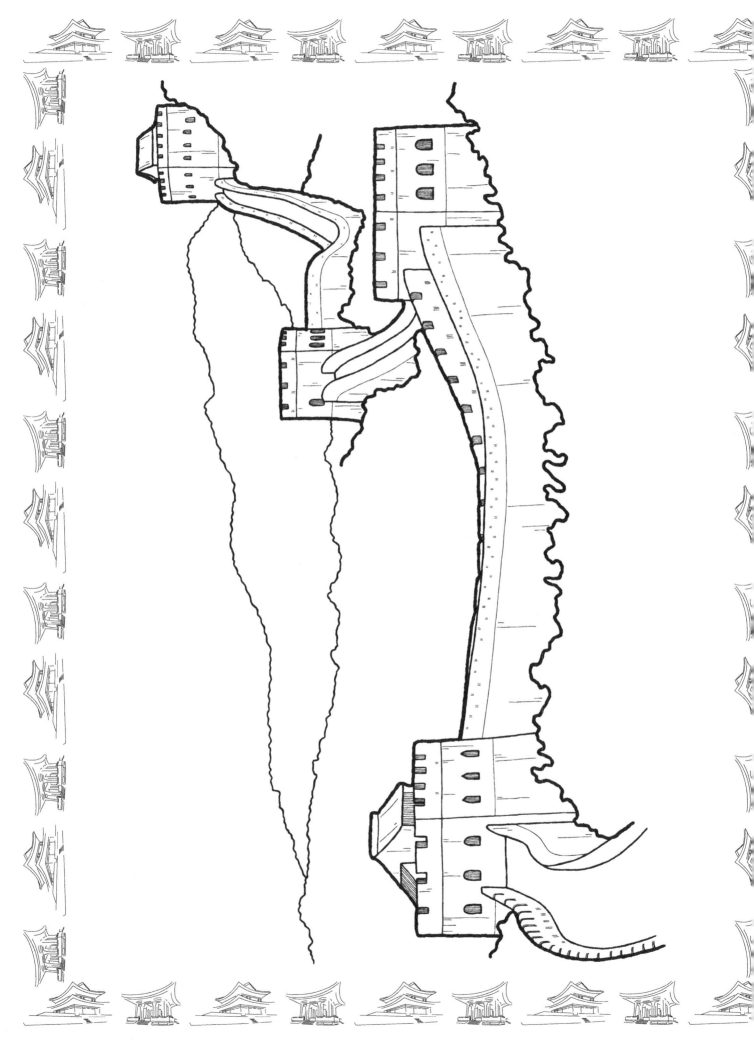

This is a Bleed Through Page If You Are Using a Coloring Marker or Pen!

Bold Illustrations
COLORING BOOKS

This is a Bleed Through Page If You Are Using a Coloring Marker or Pen!

Bold Illustrations
COLORING BOOKS

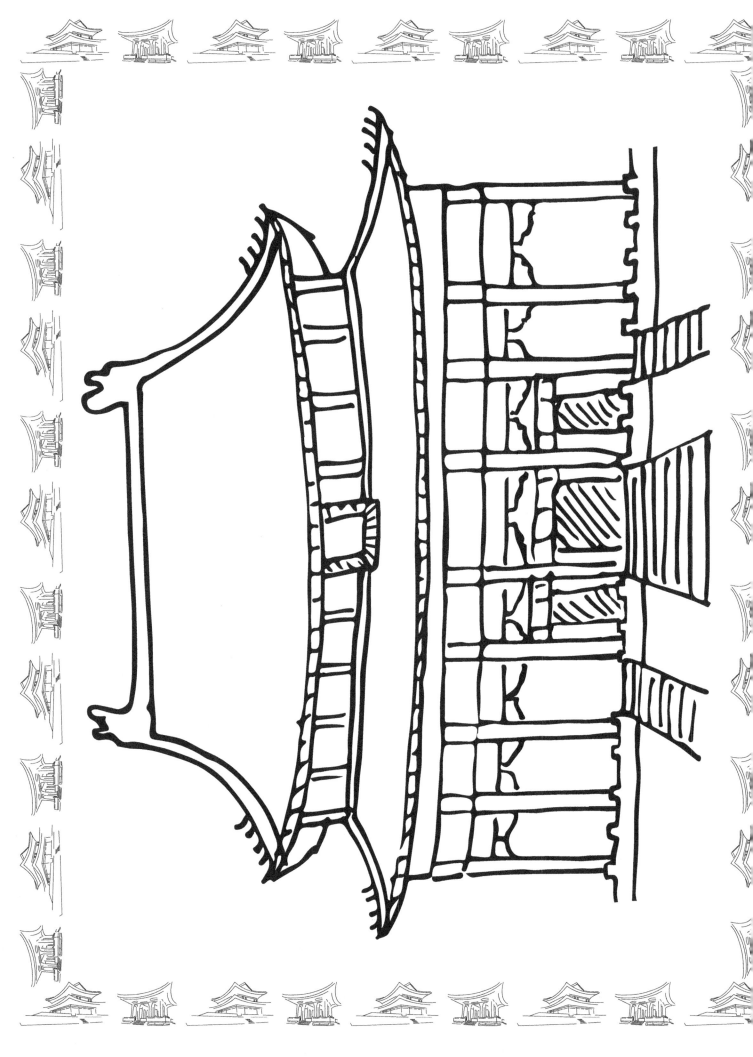

This is a Bleed Through Page If You Are Using a Coloring Marker or Pen!

Bold Illustrations
COLORING BOOKS

Bold Illustrations
COLORING BOOKS

Bold Illustrations

COLORING BOOKS

This is a Bleed Through Page If You Are Using a Coloring Marker or Pen!

Bold Illustrations
COLORING BOOKS

This is a Bleed Through Page If You Are Using a Coloring Marker or Pen!

Bold Illustrations
COLORING BOOKS

This is a Bleed Through Page If You Are Using a Coloring Marker or Pen!

Bold Illustrations
COLORING BOOKS

This is a Bleed Through Page If You Are Using a Coloring Marker or Pen!

Bold Illustrations
COLORING BOOKS

This is a Bleed Through Page If You Are Using a Coloring Marker or Pen!

Bold Illustrations
COLORING BOOKS

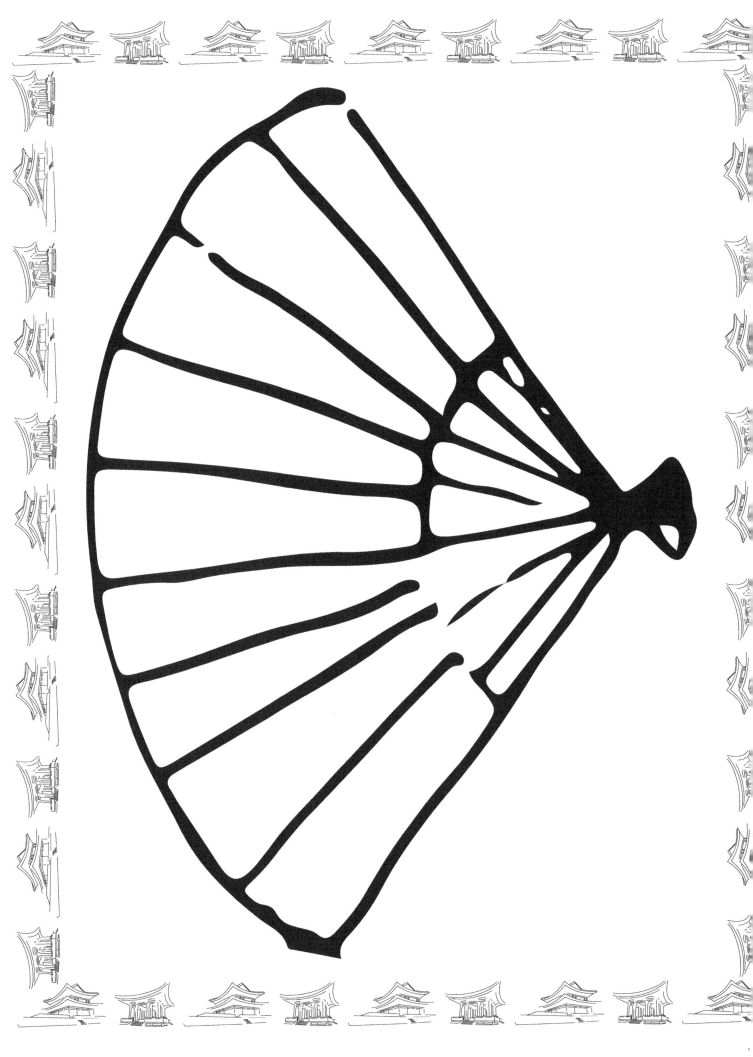

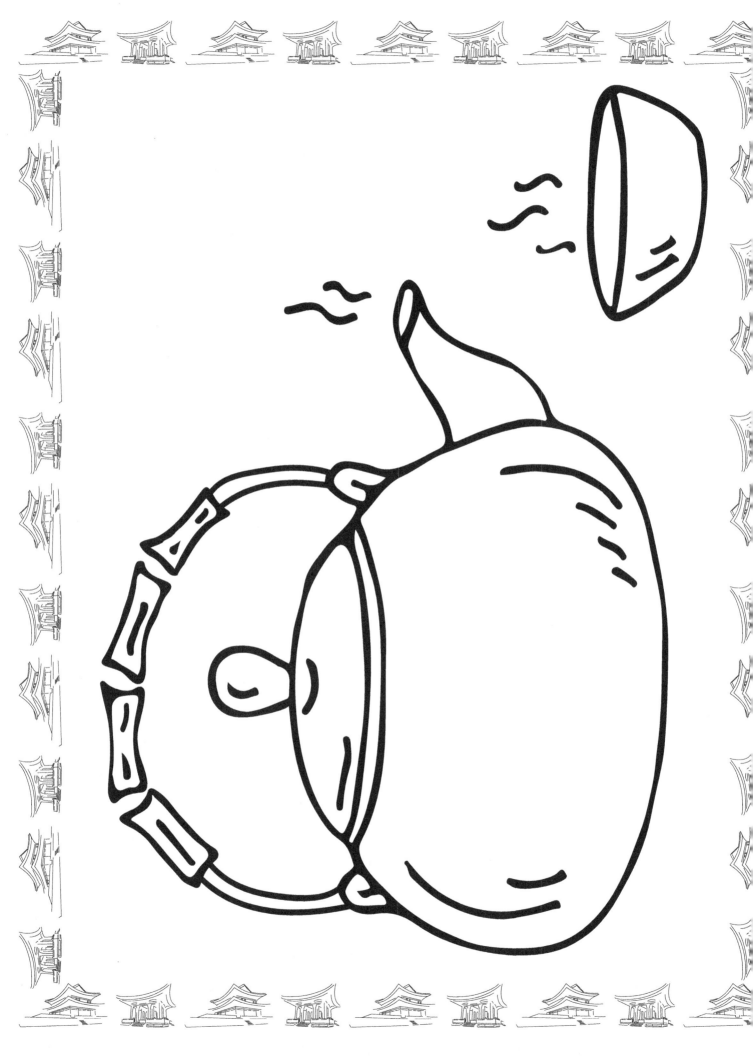

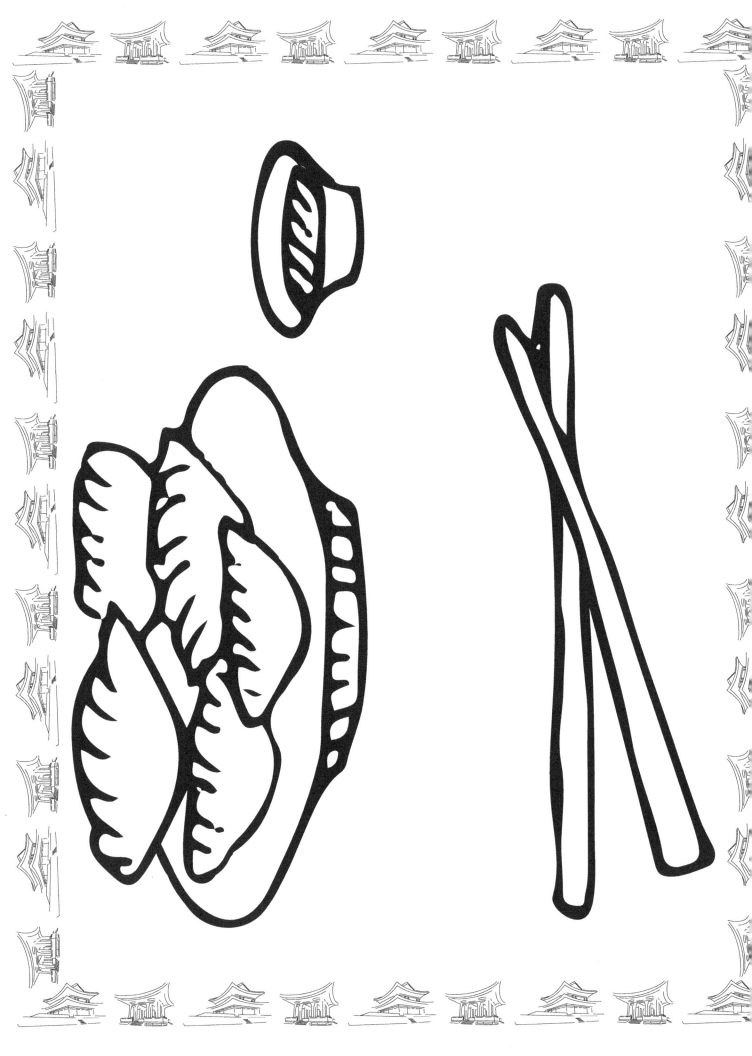

This is a Bleed Through Page If You Are Using a Coloring Marker or Pen!

Bold Illustrations
COLORING BOOKS

Made in the USA
Coppell, TX
16 March 2020